S

There is no poet so attuned to childhood as Walter de la Mare, who himself affirmed that 'the chief purpose of poetry is to give delight', and we are proud to think that this book will give every child the chance of having his own collection of de la Mare's work.

Most of the poems in these pages are like a warm private conversation with the reader. Some jolly ones can be read aloud for general pleasure, but many are best of all read quietly and alone. Then the world is transformed into a land of promise where:

> Heart bids mind
> Wonder
> Mind bids heart
> Ponder.

Margery Gill's enchanting drawings were made especially for this Puffin.

For every age and every mood

WALTER DE LA MARE

Secret Laughter

SELECTED BY ELEANOR GRAHAM

Illustrated by Margery Gill

PENGUIN BOOKS

Penguin Books Ltd, Harmondsworth, Middlesex, England
Penguin Books Australia Ltd, Ringwood, Victoria, Australia

—

The poems were first published by Faber & Faber Ltd
Published in Puffin Books as *Poems*, 1962
Reprinted 1965
Reissued as *Secret Laughter* (with additional poems) 1969
Reprinted 1970

—

Copyright © Estate of Walter de la Mare, 1969

—

Made and printed in Great Britain by
Cox & Wyman Ltd,
London, Reading and Fakenham
Set in Monotype Bembo

Contents

6. *'Look out of your Window, Mrs Gill'*

7. *Then and Now*

8. *Winter at the Doors of Spring*

9. *Secret Laughter*

LOOK THY LAST
ON ALL THINGS LOVELY
EVERY HOUR

ONE of the tremendously exciting things about Walter de la Mare's poetry is the way it lights up the reader's own experiences by the clearness and strength of the poet's vision. Memories long forgotten, or overlaid by others, suddenly return to life in all their original brilliance of colour and detail, to almost double the joy of the poems. It happens with even such simple things as a flower or the colour of freshly dug earth; the sight of a horse grazing under the midday sun, his shadow falling beneath him; or an empty house still haunted by the ghosts of former tenants – or even the sight of a small black house fly, so often killed without one questioning thought for its private life and being.

The quality of Walter de la Mare's looking was rare and remarkable. Perhaps the most quoted line of all his work is *Look thy last on all things lovely every hour* – and from it flashes a picture of him looking at the world to remember, for ever, each smallest thing, his eyes searching each object as though it might be the last they ever rested on in this life. He left another picture too, which let one see what was involved in that 'last-looking'. In *Two Deep Clear Eyes*, he says:

> *Eyes bid ears*
> *Hark:*

Ears bid eyes
Mark:
Heart bids mind
Wonder:
Mind bids heart
Ponder.

Throughout his writings de la Mare often refers to the looking, wondering, pondering which are necessary for true understanding. Sometimes he uses the word 'scrutinizing' instead of looking or gazing. Having achieved what he could by sight, he went on to wonder, using imagination and intuition to work his way into the life of what he was examining, then pondering what his senses had collected in the full light of mind and reason. Thus he came indeed to the heart of things, to the centre of being where – who can doubt it? – he found truth; truth and beauty hand in hand.

It is not possible to read Walter de la Mare's poems without becoming aware of his intense feeling for truth. And it was because of this that he was able to trust his imagination to explore and extend what his sight had already told him. His imagination, we can see for ourselves, *ran true*, as what he wrote also *rings true*.

His truth-seeking was not a process of scientific analysis and dissection – it was a creative matter, for the poet was dealing always with the things of the spirit which cannot be measured and weighed in balances.

Somewhere in *Early One Morning*, he has written that to share a child's experience one must be prepared to *occupy* the small body of the child, or to *enter* the child's mind. These things he understood well, and he could equally put himself into the body of bird, beast, or flower, fly, cat, mouse, or dog. It was never his way to preach or moralise, but he does powerfully stimulate responsible thinking – as for instance in his poem *Poor Bird*.

> *Poor bird! –*
> *No hands, no fingers thine;*
> *Two angel-coloured wings instead:*
> *But where are mine?*
>
> *Cold voiceless fish! –*
> *No hands, no spindly legs, no toes;*
> *But fins and a tail,*
> *And a mouth for nose.*
>
> *Wild weed! –*
> *Not even an eye with which to see!*
> *Or ear, or tongue,*
> *For sigh or song;*
> *Or heart to beat,*
> *Or mind to long.*
>
> *And yet – ah, would that I,*
> *In sun and shade, like thee,*
> *Might no less gentle, sweet,*
> *And lovely be.*

Always more aware than others of what lies beneath the surface of the things we know so well, he delighted in presenting us with ideas to consider for ourselves –

such as the things that make up that individuality which is oneself from the cradle to the grave, and that was his subject in *Me* – which begins:

> As long as I live
> I shall always be
> My Self – and no other
> Just me.

And, from another angle, he presented the same problem in the odd case of *Miss T.* – that

> It's a very odd thing –
> As odd as can be –
> That whatever Miss T. eats,
> Turns into Miss T.

He had a grave respect for the minds of children and for their personal dignity. He observed them closely, noting their behaviour and reactions, but not as critic, nor wishing to change them; only to discover and understand.

Belief in a child's natural goodness of heart may have inspired the verse

> Hi! handsome hunting man
> Fire your little gun.
> Bang! Now the animal
> Is dead and dumb and gone.
> Nevermore to peep again, creep again, leap again,
> Eat or sleep or drink again. Oh what fun!

Surely after reading it, the death of any little creature must always be felt as much more than the breaking of a doll. But he makes the point by direct means, without any shadow of reproof or accusation.

In the Notes to his anthology *Come Hither*, Walter de la Mare wrote: 'At every reading of a poem, though it may have been familiar from early childhood, some hitherto hidden delicacy of rhythm or intonation may be revealed. Indeed, what is read on the printed page is merely so many words. It is the reader alone who out of them can create a *poem*, and this poem changes for him as he himself changes with the years.'

So, these poems of his, which are offered specially to the young, are poems to remember all your lives. Poems to return to constantly, discovering each time how they expand in what they yield to you. Even if you keep them in mind from now until you are old, the chances are you will never find their beauty fade nor their truth tarnish.

ELEANOR GRAHAM

1

Gone the snowdrop — comes the crocus

COME – GONE
PRECIOUS STONES
SEEDS
HIDE AND SEEK
EVER
SUMMER EVENING
THE BEES' SONG
SHADOWS
MRS EARTH
APPLE-FALL
THE HOLLY
TREES
WINTER EVENING

COME - GONE

Gone the snowdrop – comes the crocus;
With the tulip blows the squill;
Jonquil white as wax between them,
And the nid-nod daffodil.

Peach, plum, cherry, pear and apple,
Rain-sweet lilac on the spray;
Come the dog-rose in the hedges –
Gone's the sweetness of the may.

PRECIOUS STONES

Ruby, amethyst, emerald, diamond,
Sapphire, sardonyx, fiery-eyed carbuncle,
    Jacynth, jasper, crystal a-sheen;
Topaz, turquoise, tourmaline, opal,
      Beryl, onyx and aquamarine: –
Marvel, O mortal! – their hue, lustre, loveliness,
Pure as a flower when its petals unfurl –
Peach-red carnelian, apple-green chrysoprase,
    Amber and coral and orient pearl!

The seeds I sowed –
For weeks unseen –
Have pushed up pygmy
Shoots of green;
So frail you'd think
The tiniest stone
Would never let
A glimpse be shown.
But no; a pebble
Near them lies,
At least a cherry-stone
In size,
Which that mere sprout
Has heaved away,
To bask in sunshine,
See the day.

Hide and seek, says the Wind,
  In the shade of the woods;
Hide and seek, says the Moon,
  To the hazel buds;
Hide and seek, says the Cloud,
  Star on to star;
Hide and seek, says the Wave
  At the harbour bar;
Hide and seek, say I,
  To myself, and step
Out of the dream of Wake
  Into the dream of Sleep.

Ever, ever
Stir and shiver
The reeds and rushes
By the river:
Ever, ever,
As if in dream,
The lone moon's silver
Sleeks the stream.
What old sorrow,
What lost love,
Moon, reeds, rushes,
Dream you of ?

SUMMER EVENING

The sandy cat by the Farmer's chair
Mews at his knee for dainty fare;
Old Rover in his moss-greened house
Mumbles a bone, and barks at a mouse.
In the dewy fields the cattle lie
Chewing the cud 'neath a fading sky;
Dobbin at manger pulls his hay:
Gone is another summer's day.

THE BEES' SONG

Thousandz of thornz there be
On the Rozez where gozez
The Zebra of Zee:
Sleek, striped, and hairy,
The steed of the Fairy
Princess of Zee.

Heavy with blossomz be
The Rozez that growzez
In the thickets of Zee.
Where grazez the Zebra,
Marked *Abracadeeebra*
Of the Princess of Zee.

And he nozez the poziez
Of the Rozez that growzez
So luvez'm and free,
With an eye, dark and wary,
In search of a Fairy,
Whose Rozez he knowzez
Were not honeyed for he,
But to breathe a sweet incense
To solace the Princess
Of far-away Zzzee.

The horse in the field,
The cows in the meadow,
Each browses and swishes
Plumb over its shadow –

It is noon. . . And beneath
That old thorn on the steep
A shepherd and sheepdog
Sit watching their sheep.

It is cool by the hedgerow,
A thorn for a tent,
Her flowers a snowdrift,
The air sweet with scent.

But oh, see already
The shade has begun
To incline to'rds the East,
As the earth and the sun

Change places, like dancers
In dance: for at morn
They stretched to the West –
When the new day was born.

MRS EARTH

Mrs Earth makes silver black,
   Mrs Earth makes iron red,
But Mrs Earth cannot stain gold
   Nor ruby red.
Mrs Earth the slenderest bone,
   Whitens in her bosom cold,
But Mrs Earth can change my dreams
   No more than ruby or gold.
Mrs Earth and Mr Sun
   Can tan my skin, and tire my toes,
But all that I'm thinking of, ever shall think,
   Why, neither knows.

Rosy the blossom that breaks in May;
    Autumn brings the apple;
Jackdaws in the belfry tower,
    Jackdaws in the steeple.
Comes a wind, blows a wind,
    Headlong down they tumble;
But bloom and berry share the sprig
    Of the prickly bramble.

THE HOLLY

The sturdiest of forest-trees
With acorns is inset;
Wan white blossoms the elder brings
To fruit as black as jet;
But O, in all green English woods
Is aught so fair to view
As the sleek, sharp, dark-leaved holly tree
And its berries burning through?

Towers the ash; and dazzling green
The larch her tassels wears;
Wondrous sweet are the clots of may
The tangled hawthorn bears;
But O, in heath or meadow or wold
Springs aught beneath the blue
As brisk and trim as a holly-tree bole
With its berries burning through?

When hither, thither, falls the snow,
And blazes small the frost,
Naked amid the winter stars
The elm's vast boughs are tossed;
But O, of all that summer showed
What now to winter's true
As the prickle-beribbed dark holly tree,
With its berries burning through!

TREES

Of all the trees in England,
    Her sweet three corners in,
Only the Ash, the bonnie Ash
    Burns fierce while it is green.

Of all the trees in England,
    From sea to sea again,
The Willow loveliest stoops her boughs
    Beneath the driving rain.

Of all the trees in England,
    Past frankincense and myrrh,
There's none for smell, of bloom and smoke,
    Like Lime and Juniper.

Of all the trees in England,
    Oak, Elder, Elm and Thorn,
The Yew alone burns lamps of peace
    For them that lie forlorn.

WINTER EVENING

Over the wintry fields the snow drifts, falling, falling,
Its frozen burden filling each hollow. And hark,
Out of the naked woods a wild bird calling,
On the starless verge of the dark.

2

Myself – and no other

ME
TWO DEEP CLEAR EYES
THE CUPBOARD
GRACE
'POOR BIRD'
WON'T
I CAN'T ABEAR
BUNCHES OF GRAPES
MISS T.
UNSTOOPING

As long as I live
I shall always be
My Self – and no other,
Just me.

Like a tree –
Willow, elder,
Aspen, thorn,
Or cypress forlorn.

Like a flower,
For its hour –
Primrose, or pink,

Or a violet –
Sunned by the sun,
And with dewdrops wet.

Always just me.
Till the day come on
When I leave this body,
It's all then done.
And the spirit within it
Is gone.

B

Two deep clear eyes,
Two ears, a mouth, a nose,
Ten supple fingers,
And ten nimble toes,
Two hands, two feet, two arms, two legs,
And a heart through which love's blessing flows.

Eyes bid ears
Hark:
Ears bid eyes
Mark:
Mouth bids nose
Smell:
Nose says to mouth,
I will:
Heart bids mind
Wonder:
Mind bids heart
Ponder.

Arms, hands, feet, legs,
Work, play, stand, walk;
And a jimp little tongue in a honey-sweet mouth
With rows of teeth due North and South,
Does nothing but talk, talk, talk.

THE
CUPBOARD

I know a little cupboard,
With a teeny tiny key,
And there's a jar of Lollipops
    For me, me, me.

It has a little shelf, my dear,
As dark as dark can be,
And there's a dish of Banbury Cakes
    For me, me, me.

I have a small fat grandmamma,
With a very slippery knee,
And she's Keeper of the Cupboard,
    With the key, key, key.

And when I'm very good, my dear,
As good as good can be,
There's Banbury Cakes, and Lollipops
    For me, me, me.

GRACE

For every sip the Hen says grace;
The Rabbit twinkles his small face;
Ev'n to the Fox, stol'n safely home,
A crafty grin of thanks must come;
Even the Spider, plump in net,
His manners cannot quite forget,
And when he's supped upon a fly
Puts what is over neatly by.
Oh, *any* one with tongue and wits
Who crowded up with victuals sits
Through breakfasts, luncheons, dinners, teas,
With never a *Thank you* or a *Please*,
Eating not what he should but can,
Can *not* be a well-mannered man.

No doubt if Cows and Sheep were able
To draw their chairs up to the table,
It's only common sense to say
They'd keep on stuffing there all day,
They need such quantities of hay.
But though they never could let pass
A dainty dish of greens or grass,
Even the littlest Lambkin would
Express a sheepish gratitude;
While sager beasts, however staid,
Might smile upon the parlourmaid.

'POOR BIRD'

Poor bird! –
No hands, no fingers thine;
Two angel-coloured wings instead:
But where are mine?

Cold voiceless fish! –
No hands, no spindly legs, no toes;
But fins and a tail,
And a mouth for nose.

Wild weed! –
Not even an eye with which to see!
Or ear, or tongue,
For sigh or song;
Or heart to beat,
Or mind to long.

And yet – ah, would that I,
In sun and shade, like thee,
Might no less gentle, sweet,
And lovely be!

WON'T

See, Master Proud-Face!
Cold as a stone;
Light, life, love
From his bright eyes gone;
Pale as a pudding
His smooth round cheek;
His head like a block
On his stiff, wooden neck.

Won't, says his cherry mouth;
Won't, says his chin;
Won't, says the Spectre,
His bosom within;
Won't, says his clenched fist;
Won't, says his foot;
Every single inch of him
Shouts, I will *NOT!* . . . .

Poor, poor Mamma –
She mopes in her room,
Pining and pining
For the moment to come
When her short sharp you *SHALL!*
She can safely unsay,
And the sun sparkle out,
And the tears dry away;

Yes, her whole heart is sighing
In passionate trust
For a kiss from those *Won'ts*
To make hay of her Must!

I CAN'T ABEAR

I can't abear a Butcher,
  I can't abide his meat,
The ugliest shop of all is his,
  The ugliest in the street;
Bakers' are warm, cobblers' dark,
  Chemists' burn watery lights;
But oh, the sawdust butcher's shop,
  That ugliest of sights!

'Bunches of grapes,' says Timothy;
'Pomegranates pink,' says Elaine;
'A junket of cream and a cranberry tart
    For me,' says Jane.

'Love-in-a-mist,' says Timothy;
'Primroses pale,' says Elaine;
'A nosegay of pinks and mignonette
    For me,' says Jane.

'Chariots of gold,' says Timothy;
'Silvery wings,' says Elaine;
'A bumpity ride in a wagon of hay
    For me,' says Jane.

MISS T.

It's a very odd thing –
   As odd as can be –
That whatever Miss T. eats
   Turns into Miss T.;
Porridge and apples,
   Mince, muffins, and mutton,
Jam, junket, jumbles –
   Not a rap, not a button
It matters; the moment
   They're out of her plate,
Though shared by Miss Butcher
   And sour Mr Bate;
Tiny and cheerful,
   And neat as can be,
Whatever Miss T. eats
   Turns into Miss T.

Low on his fours the Lion
    Treads with the surly Bear;
But Men straight upward from the dust
    Walk with their heads in air;
The free sweet winds of heaven,
    The sunlight from on high
Beat on their clear bright cheeks and brows
    As they go striding by;
The doors of all their houses
    They arch so they may go,
Uplifted o'er the four-foot beasts,
    Unstooping, to and fro.

3
Nobody, nobody told me

Eeka, Neeka, Leeka, Lee –
Here's a lock without a key;
Bring a lantern bring a candle,
Here's a door without a handle;
Shine, shine, you old thief Moon,
Here's a door without a room;
Not a whisper, moth or mouse,
Key – lock – door – room: where's the house?

Say nothing, creep away,
And live to knock another day!

SOME ONE

Some one came knocking
  At my wee small door;
Some one came knocking,
  I'm sure – sure – sure;
I listened, I opened,
  I looked to left and right,
But nought there was a-stirring
  In the still dark night;
Only the busy beetle
  Tap-tapping in the wall,
Only from the forest
  The screech-owl's call,
Only the cricket whistling
  While the dewdrops fall,
So I know not who came knocking,
  At all, at all, at all.

UNDER THE ROSE

(*The Song of the Wanderer*)

Nobody, nobody told me
What nobody, nobody knows:
But now I know where the Rainbow ends,
I know where there grows
A Tree that's called the Tree of Life,
I know where there flows
The River of All-Forgottenness,
And where the Lotus blows,
And I – I've trodden the forest, where
In flames of gold and rose,
To burn and then arise again,
     The Phoenix goes.

Nobody, nobody told me
What nobody, nobody knows;
Hide thy face in a veil of light,
Put on thy silver shoes,
Thou art the Stranger I know best,
Thou art the sweet heart, who
Came from the Land between Wake and Dream,
Cold with the morning dew.

'Grill me some bones,' said the Cobbler,
  'Some bones, my pretty Sue;
I'm tired of my lonesome with heels and soles,
Springsides and uppers too;
A mouse in the wainscot is nibbling;
A wind in the keyhole drones;
And a sheet webbed over my candle, Susie, –
  Grill me some bones!'

'Grill me some bones,' said the Cobbler,
  'I sat at my tic-tac-to;
And a footstep came to my door and stopped,
And a hand groped to and fro;
And I peered up over my boot and last;
And my feet went cold as stones: –
I saw an eye at the keyhole, Susie! –
  Grill me some bones!'

FIVE EYES

In Hans' old Mill his three black cats
Watch his bins for the thieving rats.
Whisker and claw, they crouch in the night,
Their five eyes smouldering green and bright:
Squeaks from the flour sacks, squeaks from where
The cold wind stirs on the empty stair,
Squeaking and scampering, everywhere.
Then down they pounce, now in, now out,
At whisking tail and sniffing snout;
While lean old Hans he snores away
Till peep of light at break of day;
Then up he climbs to his creaking mill,
Out come his cats all grey with meal –
Jekkel, and Jessup, and one-eyed Jill.

Twinkum, twankum, twirlum and twitch –
My great grandam – She was a Witch.
Mouse in wainscot, Saint in niche –
My great grandam – She was a Witch;
Deadly nightshade flowers in a ditch –
My great grandam – She was a Witch;
Long though the shroud, it grows stitch by stitch –
My great grandam – She was a Witch;
Wean your weakling before you breech –
My great grandam – She was a Witch;
The fattest pig's but a double flitch –
My great grandam – She was a Witch;
Nightjars rattle, owls scritch –
My great grandam – She was a Witch.

   Pretty and small,
   A mere nothing at all,
   Pinned up sharp in the ghost of a shawl,
   She'd straddle her down to the kirkyard wall
   And mutter and whisper and call,
   And call. . . .

Red blood out and black blood in,
My Nannie says I'm a child of sin.
How did I choose me my witchcraft kin?
Know I as soon as dark's dreams begin
Snared is my heart in a nightmare's gin;
Never from terror I out may win;
So dawn and dusk I pine, peak, thin,
Scarcely knowing t'other from which –
My great grandam – She was a Witch.

LISTEN!

Quiet your faces; be crossed every thumb;
Fix on me deep your eyes;
And out of my mind a story shall come,
Old, and lovely, and wise.

Old as the pebbles that fringe the cold seas,
Lovely as apples in rain;
Wise as the King who learned of the bees,
Then learned of the emmets again.

Old as the fruits that in mistletoe shine ;
Lovely as amber, as snow;
Wise as the fool who when care made to pine
Cried, Hey and fol lol, lilly lo !

Old as the woods rhyming Thomas snuffed sweet,
When pillion he rode with the Queen:
Lovely as elf-craft; wise as the street
Where the roofs of the humble are seen. . . .

Ay, there's a stirring, there's wind in the bough;
Hearken, a harp I hear ring:
Like a river of water my story shall flow
Like linnets of silver sing.

'*Applecumjockaby*, blindfold eye!
How many rooks come sailing by,
Caw – caw, in the deep blue sky?'

'*Applecumjockaby, you* tell me!
I can listen though I can't see;
Twenty soot-black rooks there be.'

'*Applecumjockaby*, I say, No!
Who can tell what he don't know?
Blindman's in, and round we go.'

With this round glass
I can make *Magic* talk –
A myriad shells show
In a scrap of chalk;

Of but an inch of moss
A forest – flowers and trees;
A drop of water
Like a hive of bees.

I lie in wait and watch
How the deft spider jets
The woven web-silk
From his spinnerets;

The tigerish claws he has!
And oh! the silly flies
That stumble into his net –
With all those eyes!

Not even the tiniest thing
But this my glass
Will make more marvellous,
And itself surpass.

Yes, and with lenses like it,
Eyeing the moon,
'Twould seem you'd walk there
In an afternoon!

A very, very old house I know –
And ever so many people go,
Past the small lodge, forlorn and still,
Under the heavy branches, till
Comes the blank wall, and there's the door,
Go in they do; come out no more.
No voice says aught; no spark of light
Across that threshold cheers the sight;
Only the evening star on high
Less lonely makes a lonely sky,
As, one by one, the people go
Into that very old house I know.

Some one is always sitting there,
                    In the little green orchard;
    Even when the sun is high,
    In noon's unclouded sky,
    And faintly droning goes
    The bee from rose to rose,
Some one in shadow is sitting there,
                    In the little green orchard.

Yes, and when twilight's falling softly
                    On the little green orchard;
    When the grey dew distils
    And every flower-cup fills;
    When the last blackbird says,
    'What – what!' and goes her way – ssh!
I have heard voices calling softly
                    In the little green orchard.

Not that I am afraid of being there,
                    In the little green orchard;
    Why, when the moon's been bright,
    Shedding her lonesome light,
    And moths like ghosties come,
    And the horned snail leaves home:
I've sat there, whispering and listening there,
                    In the little green orchard;

Only it's strange to be feeling there,
          In the little green orchard;
    Whether you paint or draw,
    Dig, hammer, chop, or saw;
    When you are most alone,
    All but the silence gone . . .
Some one is waiting and watching there,
          In the little green orchard.

THE HOUSE

A lane at the end of Old Pilgrim Street
Leads on to a sheep-track over the moor,
Till you come at length to where two streams meet,
The brook called Liss, and the shallow Stour.

Their waters mingle and sing all day –
Rushes and kingcups, rock and stone;
And aloof in the valley, forlorn and grey,
Is a house whence even the birds have flown.

Its ramshackle gate swings crazily; but
No sickle covets its seeding grass;
There's a cobbled path to a door close-shut;
But no face shows at the window-glass.

No smoke wreathes up in the empty air
From the chimney over its weed-green thatch;
Briar and bryony ramble there;
And no thumb tirls at the broken latch.

Even the warbling water seems
To make lone music for none to hear;
Else is a quiet found only in dreams,
And in dreams this foreboding, though not of fear.

Yes, often at dusk-fall when nearing home –
The hour of the crescent and evening star –
Again to the bridge and the streams I come,
Where the sedge and the rushes and kingcups are:

And I stand, and listen, and sigh – in vain;
Since only of Fancy's the face I see;
Yet its eyes in the twilight on mine remain,
And it seems to be craving for company.

LONE

Shrill rang the squeak in the empty house
Of the sharp-nosed mouse, the hungry mouse.

'Sing, sing: here none doth dwell!'
Dripped the water in the well.

A robin on the shepherd's grave
Whistled a solitary stave.

And, 'Lone-lone!' the curlew cried,
Scolding the sheep-strewn mountain's side.

Who said, 'Peacock Pie'?
  The old King to the sparrow:
Who said, 'Crops are ripe'?
  Rust to the harrow:
Who said, 'Where sleeps she now?
  Where rests she now her head,
Bathed in eve's loveliness'?
  That's what I said.

Who said, 'Ay, mum's the word'?
  Sexton to willow:
Who said 'Green dusk for dreams,
  Moss for a pillow'?
Who said, 'All Time's delight
  Hath she for narrow bed;
Life's troubled bubble broken'? –
  That's what I said.

4

Round Man's Winter Fire

TOM'S LITTLE DOG

Tom told his dog called Tim to beg,
And up at once he sat,
His two clear amber eyes fixed fast,
His haunches on his mat.

Tom poised a lump of sugar on
His nose; then, 'Trust!' says he;
Stiff as a guardsman sat his Tim;
Never a hair stirred he.

'Paid for!' says Tom; and in a trice
Up jerked that moist black nose;
A snap of teeth, a crunch, a munch,
And down the sugar goes!

THE BANDOG

Has anybody seen my Mopser? –
  A comely dog is he,
With hair of the colour of a Charles the Fifth,
  And teeth like ships at sea,
His tail it curls straight upwards,
  His ears stand two abreast,
And he answers to the simple name of Mopser,
  When civilly addressed.

Sweet Peridarchus was a Prince,
The Prince he was of – Mouses;
He roved and roamed the haunts of Men,
And ranged about their houses.

He gnawed his way along a street,
Through holes in every wainscot,
Fandangoed in the attics and
From basement on to basement.

His eyes like bits of rubies shone;
His coat, as sleek as satin,
With teeth as sharp as needle-points
He kept to keep him fat in.

His squeak so sharp in the small hours rang
That every waker wondered;
He trimmed his whiskers stiff as wire,
Had sweethearts by the hundred.

He'd gut a Cheshire cheese with ease,
Plum cake devoured in slices,
Lard, haggis, suet, sausages,
And everything that nice is.

Cork out, he'd dangle down his tail
For oil that was in bottle;
Nothing too sweet, nothing too fat
For Peridarchus' throttle.

He'd dance upon a chimney-pot,
The merry stars a-twinkling;
Or, scampering up a chandelier,
Set all the lustres tinkling.

He'd skip into a pianoforte
To listen how it sounded;
He bored into a butt of wine,
And so was nearly drownded.

At midnight when he sat at meat,
Twelve saucy sonsy maidens,
With bee-sweet voices ditties sang,
Some sad ones, and some gay ones.

For bodyguard he had a score
Of warriors grim and hardy;
They raided every larder round,
From Peebles to Cromàrty.

Grimalkin – deep in dreams she lay,
Comes he, with these gay friskers,
Steals up and gnaws away her claws,
And plucks out all her whiskers.

He scaled a bell-rope where there snored
The Bailiff and his Lady;
Danced on his nose, nibbled her toes,
And kissed the squalling Baby.

A merry life was his, I trow,
Despite it was a short one;
One night he met a mort of rats –
He bared his teeth, and fought one:

A bully ruffian, thrice his size;
But when the conflict ended,
He sighed 'Alack, my back is broke,
And that can ne'er be mended.'

They laid him lifeless on a bier,
They lapped him up in ermine;
They lit a candle, inches thick,
His Uncle preached the sermon: –

O Mouseland, mourn for him that's gone,
Our noble Peridarchus!
In valiant fight but yesternight,
And now, alas, a carcass!

'A Hero – Mouse or Man – is one
Who never wails or winces;
Friends, shed a tear for him that's here,
The Princeliest of Princes!'

NICHOLAS NYE

Thistle and darnel and dock grew there,
   And a bush, in the corner, of may,
On the orchard wall I used to sprawl
   In the blazing heat of the day;
Half asleep and half awake,
   While the birds went twittering by,
And nobody there my lone to share
      But Nicholas Nye.

Nicholas Nye was lean and grey,
   Lame of a leg and old,
More than a score of donkey's years
   He had seen since he was foaled;
He munched the thistles, purple and spiked,
   Would sometimes stoop and sigh,
And turn his head, as if he said,
      'Poor Nicholas Nye!'

Alone with his shadow he'd drowse in the meadow,
   Lazily swinging his tail,
At break of day he used to bray, –
   Not much too hearty and hale;
But a wonderful gumption was under his skin,
   And a clear calm light in his eye,
And once in a while he'd smile . . .
      Would Nicholas Nye.

Seem to be smiling at me, he would,
  From his bush in the corner, of may, –
Bony and ownerless, widowed and worn,
  Knobble-kneed, lonely and grey;
And over the grass would seem to pass
  'Neath the deep dark blue of the sky,
Something much better than words between me
    And Nicholas Nye.

But dusk would come in the apple boughs,
  The green of the glow-worm shine,
The birds in nest would crouch to rest,
  And home I'd trudge to mine;
And there, in the moonlight, dark with dew,
  Asking not wherefore nor why,
Would brood like a ghost, and as still as a post,
    Old Nicholas Nye.

'Come!' said Old Shellover.
'What?' says Creep.
'The horny old Gardener's fast asleep;
The fat cock Thrush
To his nest has gone;

And the dew shines bright
In the rising Moon;
Old Sallie Worm from her hole doth peep:
Come!' said Old Shellover.
'Ay!' said Creep.

WHO REALLY?

When Winter's o'er, the Bear once more
Rolls from his hollow tree
And pokes about, and in and out,
Where dwells the honey-bee.
Then all the little creatures go,
And to their Queen they say:
'Here's that old Bruin, hark, what he's doing,
Let's drive the beast away!'
Old Bruin smiles, and smoothes his hair
Over a sticky nose;
'That Thieves should hate a Thief,' he smirks,
'Who really would suppose!'

MASTER RABBIT

As I was walking,
Thyme sweet to my nose,
Green grasshoppers talking,
Rose rivalling rose:

Wings clear as amber,
Outspread in the light,
As from bush to bush
The Linnet took flight:

Master Rabbit I saw
In the shadow-rimmed mouth
Of his sandy cavern
Looking out to the South.

'Twas dew-tide coming,
The turf was sweet
To nostril, curved tooth,
And wool-soft feet.

Sun was in West,
Crystal in beam
Of its golden shower
Did his round eye gleam.

Lank horror was I
And a foe, poor soul –
Snowy flit of a scut,
He was into his hole:

And – *stamp, stamp, stamp,*
Through dim labyrinths clear –
The whole world darkened:
A Human near!

All but blind
  In his chambered hole
Gropes for worms
  The four-clawed Mole.

All but blind
  In the evening sky
The hooded Bat
  Twirls softly by.

All but blind
  In the burning day
The Barn-Owl blunders
  On her way.

And blind as are
  These three to me,
So, blind to Some-One
  I must be.

How large unto the tiny fly
  Must little things appear ! –
A rosebud like a featherbed,
  Its prickle like a spear;

A dewdrop like a looking-glass,
  A hair like golden wire;
The smallest grain of mustard-seed
  As fierce as coals of fire;

A loaf of bread, a lofty hill;
  A wasp, a cruel leopard;
And specks of salt as bright to see
  As lambkins to a shepherd.

HI!

Hi! handsome hunting man
Fire your little gun.
Bang! Now the animal
Is dead and dumb and done.
Nevermore to peep again, creep again, leap again,
Eat or sleep or drink again. Oh, what fun!

DONE FOR

Old Ben Bailey
He's been and done
For a small brown bunny
With his long gun.

Glazed are the eyes
That stared so clear,
And no sound stirs
In that hairy ear.

What was once beautiful
Now breathes not,
Bound for Ben Bailey's
Smoking pot.

There was a ship of Rio
    Sailed out into the blue,
And nine and ninety monkeys
    Were all her jovial crew.
From bo'sun to the cabin boy,
    From quarter to caboose,
There weren't a stitch of calico
    To breech 'em – tight or loose;
From spar to deck, from deck to keel,
    From barnacle to shroud,
There weren't one pair of reach-me-downs
    To all that jabbering crowd.
But wasn't it a gladsome sight,
    When roared the deep-sea gales,
To see them reef her fore and aft,
    A-swinging by their tails!
Oh, wasn't it a gladsome sight,
    When glassy calm did come,
To see them squatting tailor-wise
    Around a keg of rum!
Oh, wasn't it a gladsome sight,
    When in she sailed to land,
To see them all a-scampering skip
    For nuts across the sand!

PUSS

Puss loves man's winter fire
Now that the sun so soon
Leaves the hours cold it warmed
In burning June.

She purrs full length before
The heaped-up hissing blaze,
Drowsy in slumber down
Her head she lays.

While he with whom she dwells
Sits snug in his inglenook,
Stretches his legs to the flames
And reads his book.

Call the cows home!
Call the cows home!
Louring storm clouds
Hitherward come;
East to West
Their wings are spread;
Lost in the blue
Is each heaven-high head;
They've dimmed the sun;
Turned day to night;
With a whistling wind
The woods are white;
Down streams the rain
On farm, barn, byre,
Bright green hill,
And bramble and brier,
Filling the valley
With glimmer and gloom:
Call the cows home!
Call the cows home!

5

Polly, spare a crumb

ALAS, ALACK!

Ann, Ann!
  Come! quick as you can!
There's a fish that *talks*
  In the frying-pan.
Out of the fat,
  As clear as glass,
He put up his mouth
  And moaned 'Alas!'
Oh, most mournful,
  'Alas, alack!'
Then turned to his sizzling,
  And sank him back.

MARY

Mary! Mary! *Mary!*
Come to the dairy, please!
Give me some butter to spread on my bread,
Give me a morsel of cheese.
The cows in the meadow are chewing the cud,
Some of them deep in the stream –
Give me a suppet of curds and whey,
Or a wee little bowl of cream!

It's half a week since breakfast,
And cook won't spare a crumb;
Fol-di-diddle-O, starve I shall,
Unless, you dear, you come!
A hungry wolf's inside me,
Though I wouldn't for worlds just tease:
Mary! Mary! *Mary!*
Come to the dairy, *please!*

Monkeys in a forest,
Beggarmen in rags,
Marrow in a knucklebone,
Gold in leather bags;

Dumplings in the oven,
Fishes in a pool,
Flowers in a parlour,
Dunces in a school;

Feathers in a pillow,
Cattle in a shed,
Honey in a beehive,
        And Babs in bed.

Ah, would I were a pastrycook!
My Mopsa then I'd make
A Sallie Lunn, a Crumpet, and a
      Cake.

Ah, would I were a Grocer!
How happy she would be
With Jars of Honey, Raisins, Currants,
      Tea.

Ah, would I were an Oilman!
She should never, never mope
For Clothes Pegs, Candles, Soda, or for
      Soap.

Ah, would I were a Pothecary!
For Possets she'd not pine,
Or Pills, or Ipecacuanha
      Wine.

Or, just suppose, a Fishmonger!
The *pains* I would be at
To pick her out a Whitebait, or a
      Sprat!

Or a green-baize-aproned Fruiterer –
The punnets that should come
Of Cherries, Apples, Peach, and Pear, and
    Plum!

There's a small dark shop I know of too,
In another place, called Sleep;
And there's nothing sold in Dreams it doesn't
    Keep.

But as it's only rhymes I make,
I can but dower my Dove
With scribbles, and with kisses, and with
    Love.

SILLY SALLIE

Silly Sallie! Silly Sallie!
Called the boys down Blind Man's Alley;
But she, still smiling, never made
A sign she had heard, or answer gave;
Her blue eyes in her skimpy hair
Seemed not to notice they were there;
Seemed still to be watching, rain or shine,
Some other place, not out, but in:
Though it pleased the boys in Blind Man's Alley
Still to be shouting *Silly Sallie!*

Little Pollie Pillikins
Peeped into the kitchen,
'H'm,' says she, 'Ho,' says she,
    'Nobody there!'
Only little meeny mice,
Miniken and miching
On the big broad flagstones, empty and bare.

Greedy Pollie Pillikins
Crept into the pantry,
There stood an Apple Pasty,
    Sugar white as snow.
Off the shelf she toppled it,
Quick and quiet and canty,
And the meeny mice they watched her
    On her tip-tap-toe.

'Thief, Pollie Pillikins!'
Crouching in the shadows there,
Flickering in the candle-shining,
    Fee, fo, fum!
Munching up the pastry,
Crunching up the apples,
'Thief!' squeaked the smallest mouse,
    'Pollie, spare a crumb!'

Poor little Lucy
  By some mischance,
Lost her shoe
  As she did dance:
'Twas not on the stairs,
  Not in the hall;
Not where they sat
  At supper at all.
She looked in the garden,
  But there it was not;
Henhouse, or kennel,
  Or high dovecote,
Dairy and meadow,
  And wild woods through
Showed not a trace
  Of Lucy's shoe.
Bird nor bunny
  Nor glimmering moon
Breathed a whisper
  Of where 'twas gone.
It was cried and cried,
  Oyez and *Oyez!*
In French, Dutch, Latin
  And Portuguese.
Ships the dark seas
  Went plunging through,

But none brought news
   Of Lucy's shoe;
And still she patters,
   In silk and leather,
Snow, sand, shingle,
   In every weather;
Spain, and Africa,
   Hindustan,
Java, China,
   And lamped Japan,
Plain and desert,
   She hops – hops through,
Pernambuco
   To gold Peru;
Mountain and forest,
   And river too,
All the world over
   For her lost shoe.

SALLIE

When Sallie with her pitcher goes
Down the long lane where the hawthorn blows
    For water from the spring,
I watch her bobbing sun-bright hair,
In the green leaves and blossoms there,
Shining and gleaming primrose-fair;
Till back again, like bird on wing,
Her pitcher, brimmed, she turns to bring –
    Oh, what a joy to see!
And her clear voice, the birds' above,
Rings sweet with joy, entranced with love –
    Ah! would 'twere love for me!

Gold locks, and black locks,
   Red locks, and brown,
Topknot to love-curl
   The hair wisps down;
Straight above the clear eyes,
   Rounded round the ears,
Snip-snap and snick-a-snick,
   Clash the Barber's shears;
Us, in the looking-glass,
   Footsteps in the street,
Over, under, to and fro,
   The lean blades meet;
Bay Rum or Bear's Grease,
   A silver groat to pay –
Then out a-shin-shan-shining
   In the bright, blue day.

Keep me a crust
Or starve I must;
Hoard me a bone
Or I am gone;
A handful of coals
Leave red for me;
Or the smouldering log
Of a wild-wood tree;
Even a kettle
To sing on the hob
Will comfort the heart
Of poor old Lob:
Then with his hairy
Hands he'll bless
Prosperous master,
And kind mistress.

POOR HENRY

Thick in its glass
   The physic stands,
Poor Henry lifts
   Distracted hands;
His round cheek wans
   In the candlelight,
To smell that smell!
   To see that sight!

Finger and thumb
   Clinch his small nose,
A gurgle, a gasp,
   And down it goes;
Scowls Henry now;
   But mark that cheek,
Sleek with the bloom
   Of health next week!

99

6

'Look out of your Window, Mrs Gill'

DAME HICKORY
JIM JAY
THE ISLE OF LONE
THE MOCKING FAIRY
THE CORNER
THE HUNTSMEN
CAKE AND SACK
OFF THE GROUND
THE LISTENERS

'Dame Hickory, Dame Hickory,
Here's sticks for your fire,
Furze-twigs, and oak-twigs,
And beech-twigs and briar!'
But when old Dame Hickory came for to see,
She found 'twas the voice of the False Faërie.

'Dame Hickory, Dame Hickory,
Here's meat for your broth,
Goose-flesh, and hare's flesh,
And pig's trotters both!'
But when old Dame Hickory came for to see,
She found 'twas the voice of the False Faërie.

'Dame Hickory, Dame Hickory,
Here's a wolf at your door,
His teeth grinning white,
And his tongue wagging sore!'
'Nay!' said Dame Hickory, 'ye False Faërie!'
But a wolf 'twas indeed, and famished was he.

'Dame Hickory, Dame Hickory,
Here's buds for your tomb,
Bramble, and lavender,
And rosemary bloom!'
'Whsst!' sighs Dame Hickory, 'you False Faërie,
You cry like a wolf, you do, and trouble poor me.'

JIM JAY

Do diddle di do,
  Poor Jim Jay
Got stuck fast
  In Yesterday.

Squinting he was,
  On cross-legs bent,
Never heeding
  The wind was spent,
Round veered the weathercock,
  The sun drew in –
And stuck was Jim
  Like a rusty pin. . . .
We pulled and we pulled
  From seven till twelve,
Jim, too frightencd
  To help himself.
But all in vain.
  The clock struck one,
And there was Jim
  A little bit gone.
At half-past five
  You scarce could see
A glimpse of his flapping
  Handkerchee.
And when came noon,
  And we climbed sky-high,
Jim was a speck
  Slip – slipping by.
Come tomorrow,
  The neighbours say,
He'll be past crying for:
  Poor Jim Jay.

THE ISLE OF LONE

Three dwarfs there were which lived in an isle,
  And the name of that isle was Lone,
And the names of the dwarfs were Alliolyle,
  Lallerie, Muziomone.

Their house was small and sweet of the sea,
  And pale as the Malmsey wine;
Their bowls were three and their beds were three,
  And their nightcaps white were nine.

Their beds were made of the holly-wood,
  Their combs of the tortoise-shell,
Three basins of silver in corners there stood,
  And three little ewers as well.

Green rushes, green rushes lay thick on the floor,
  For light beamed a gobbet of wax;
There were three wooden stools for whatever they wore
  On their humpity-dumpity backs.

So each would lie on a drowsy pillow
  And watch the moon in the sky –
And hear the parrot scream to the billow,
  And the billow roar reply.

Parrots of sapphire and sulphur and amber,
    Amethyst, azure and green,
While apes in the palm trees would scramble and clamber,
    Hairy and hungry and lean.

All night long with bubbles a-glisten
    The ocean cried under the moon,
Till ape and parrot too sleepy to listen
    To sleep and slumber were gone.

Then from three small beds the dark hours' while
    In a house in the Island of Lone
Rose the snoring of Lallerie, Alliolyle,
    The snoring of Muziomone.

But soon as ever came peep of sun
    On coral and feathery tree,
Three night-capped dwarfs to the surf would run
    And soon were a-bob in the sea.

At six they went fishing, at nine to snare
    Young foxes in the dells,
At noon in the shade on sweet fruits would fare,
    And blew in their twisted shells.

Dark was the sea they gambolled in,
    And thick with silver fish,
Dark as green glass blown clear and thin
    To be a monarch's dish.

They sate to sup in a jasmine bower,
  Lit pale with flies of fire,
Their bowls the hue of the iris-flower,
  And lemon their attire.

Sweet wine in little cups they sipped,
  And golden honeycomb
Into their bowls of cream they dipped,
  Whipt light and white as foam.

Now Alliolyle where the sand-flower blows
  Taught three old apes to sing –
Taught three old apes to dance on their toes
  And caper round in a ring.

They yelled them hoarse and they croaked them sweet,
  They twirled them about and around,
To the noise of their voices they danced with their feet,
  They stamped with their feet on the ground.

But down to the shore skipped Lallerie,
  His parrot on his thumb,
And the twain they scritched in mockery,
  While the dancers go and come,

And, alas! in the evening, rosy and still,
  Light-haired Lallerie
Bitterly quarrelled with Alliolyle
  By the yellow-sanded sea.

The rising moon swam sweet and large
  Before their furious eyes,
And they rolled and rolled to the coral marge
  Where the surf forever cries.

Too late, too late, comes Muziomone:
  Clear in the clear green sea
Alliolyle lies not alone,
  But clasped with Lallerie.

He blows on his shell low plaintive notes;
  Ape, perequito, bee
Flock where a shoe on the salt wave floats, –
  The shoe of Lallerie.

He fetches nightcaps, one and nine,
  Grey apes he dowers three,
His house as fair as the Malmsey wine
  Seems sad as the cypress-tree.

Three bowls he brims with sweet honeycomb
  To feast the bumble-bees,
Saying, 'O bees, be this your home,
  For grief is on the seas!'

He sate him down in a coral grot,
  At the flowing in of the tide;
When ebbed the billow, there was not,
  Save coral, aught beside.

So hairy apes in three white beds,
　　And nightcaps, one and nine,
On moonlit pillows lay three heads
　　Bemused with dwarfish wine.

A tomb of coral, the dirge of bee,
　　The grey apes' guttural groan
For Alliolyle, for Lallerie,
　　For thee, O Muziomone!

THE MOCKING FAIRY

'Won't you look out of your window, Mrs Gill?'
   Quoth the Fairy, nidding, nodding in the garden;
'*Can't* you look out of your window, Mrs Gill?'
   Quoth the Fairy, laughing softly in the garden;
But the air was still, the cherry boughs were still,
And the ivy-tod 'neath the empty sill,
And never from her window looked out Mrs Gill
   On the Fairy shrilly mocking in the garden.

'What have they done with you, you poor Mrs Gill?'
   Quoth the Fairy brightly glancing in the garden;
'Where have they hidden you, you poor old Mrs Gill?'
   Quoth the Fairy dancing lightly in the garden;
But night's faint veil now wrapped the hill,
Stark 'neath the stars stood the dead-still Mill,
And out of her cold cottage never answered Mrs Gill
   The Fairy mimbling, mambling in the garden.

THE CORNER

Good News to tell!
Oh, mark it well!
Old Mister Jones,
Once all but bones –
There never was
A sight forlorner –
At last, at last
All danger past,
Has been and gone and
Turned the corner;
And every hour
Is growing younger.

A week ago,
By Almanac,
His long white beard
Went jetty black,
The red into his cheeks
Came back.
His teeth were sharp
And thirty-two,
His faded eyes
A bright bird-blue.
When two-three days
Were scarcely run,
He slips from forty
To twenty-one;
He skips and dances,
Heel and toe;

He couldn't downwards
Quicker grow.
All that he'd learned
Began to go;
His memory melted
Just like snow.

At plump four foot
He burst his stitches,
His trousers dwindled
Back to breeches;
The breeches gone,
There came short clothes,
Two dumpling cheeks,
A button nose,
A mop of curls,
Ten crinkled toes.
And now as fast
As he is able,
He's nestling down
Into his cradle.

Old Mrs Jones,
With piping eye,
She rocks, and croons
Him *Hushaby*.
Last Sunday gone,
He turned the corner,
And still grows
Younger, younger, younger . . .
Old Mister Jones.

Three jolly gentlemen,
  In coats of red,
Rode their horses
  Up to bed.

Three jolly gentlemen
  Snored till morn,
Their horses champing
  The golden corn.

Three jolly gentlemen,
  At break of day,
Came clitter-clatter down the stairs
  And galloped away.

Old King Caraway
  Supped on cake,
And a cup of sack
  His thirst to slake;
Bird in arras
  And hound in hall
Watched very softly
  Or not at all;
Fire in the middle,
  Stone all round
Changed not, heeded not,
  Made no sound;
All by himself
  At the Table High
He'd nibble and sip
  While his dreams slipped by;
And when he had finished,
  He'd nod and say,
'Cake and sack
  For King Caraway!'

Three jolly farmers
Once bet a pound
Each dance the others would
Off the ground.
Out of their coats
They slipped right soon,
And neat and nicesome,
Put each his shoon.

One – Two – Three! –
And away they go,
Not too fast,
And not too slow;
Out from the elm-tree's
Noonday shadow
Into the sun
And across the meadow.
Past the schoolroom,
With knees well bent,
Fingers a-flicking,
They dancing went.
Up sides and over,
And round and round,
They crossed click-clacking,
The Parish bound.

By Tupman's meadow
They did their mile,
Tee-to-tum
On a three-barred stile.
Then straight through Whipham,
Downhill to Week,
Footing it lightsome,
But not too quick,
Up fields to Watchet,
And on through Wye,
Till seven fine churches
They'd seen skip by –
Seven fine churches,
And five old mills,
Farms in the valley,
And sheep on the hills;
Old Man's Acre
And Dead Man's Pool
All left behind,
As they danced through Wool.

And Wool gone by,
Like tops that seem
To spin in sleep
They danced in dream:
Withy – Wellover –
Wassop – Wo –
Like an old clock
Their heels did go.

A league and a league
And a league they went,
And not one weary,
And not one spent.
And lo, and behold!
Past Willow-cum-Leigh
Stretched with its waters
The great green sea.

Says Farmer Bates,
'I puffs and I blows,
What's under the water,
Why, no man knows!'
Says Farmer Giles,
'My wind comes weak,
And a good man drownded
Is far to seek.'
But Farmer Turvey,
On twirling toes,
Up's with his gaiters,
And in he goes:
Down where the mermaids
Pluck and play
On their twangling harps
In a sea-green day;
Down where the mermaids,
Finned and fair,
Sleek with their combs
Their yellow hair . . .

Bates and Giles –
On the shingle sat,
Gazing at Turvey's
Floating hat.
But never a ripple
Nor bubble told
Where he was supping
Off plates of gold.
Never an echo
Rilled through the sea
Of the feasting and dancing
And minstrelsy.
They called – called – called:
Came no reply:
Nought but the ripples'
Sandy sigh.
Then glum and silent
They sat instead,
Vacantly brooding
On home and bed,
Till both together
Stood up and said: –
'Us knows not, dreams not,
Where you be,
Turvey, unless
In the deep blue sea;
But axcusing silver –
And it comes most willing –
Here's us two paying

Our forty shilling;
For it's sartin **sure**, Turvey,
Safe and sound,
You danced us square, Turvey,
Off the ground!'

THE LISTENERS

'Is there anybody there?' said the Traveller,
  Knocking on the moonlit door;
And his horse in the silence champed the grasses
  Of the forest's ferny floor:
And a bird flew up out of the turret,
  Above the Traveller's head:
And he smote upon the door again a second time;
  'Is there anybody there?' he said.

But no one descended to the Traveller;
  No head from the leaf-fringed sill
Leaned over and looked into his grey eyes,
  Where he stood perplexed and still.
But only a host of phantom listeners
  That dwelt in the lone house then
Stood listening in the quiet of the moonlight
  To that voice from the world of men:
Stood thronging the faint moonbeams on the dark stair,
  That goes down to the empty hall,
Hearkening in an air stirred and shaken
  By the lonely Traveller's call.
And he felt in his heart their strangeness,
  Their stillness answering his cry,
While his horse moved, cropping the dark turf,
  'Neath the starred and leafy sky;
For he suddenly smote on the door, even
  Louder, and then lifted his head: –
'Tell them I came, and no one answered,
  That I kept my word,' he said.
Never the least stir made the listeners,
  Though every word he spake
Fell echoing through the shadowiness of the still house
  From the one man left awake:
Ay, they heard his foot upon the stirrup,
  And the sound of iron on stone,
And how the silence surged softly backward,
  When the plunging hoofs were gone.

7
Then and Now

Twenty, forty, sixty, eighty,
   A hundred years ago,
All through the night with lantern bright
   The Watch trudged to and fro.
And little boys tucked snug abed
   Would wake from dreams to hear –
'Two o' the morning by the clock,
   And the stars a-shining clear!'
Or, when across the chimney-tops,
   Screamed shrill a North-East gale,
A faint and shaken voice would shout,
   'Three! – and a storm of hail!'

THE OLD STONE HOUSE

Nothing on the grey roof, nothing on the brown,
Only a little greening where the rain drips down;
Nobody at the window, nobody at the door,
Only a little hollow which a foot once wore;
But still I tread on tiptoe, still tiptoe on I go,
Past nettles, porch, and weedy well, for oh, I know
A friendless face is peering, and a clear still eye
Peeps closely through the casement as my step goes by.

There came an old sailor
Who sat to sup
Under the trees
Of the *Golden Cup*.

Beer in a mug
And a slice of cheese
With a hunk of bread
He munched at his ease.

Then in the summer
Dusk he lit
A little black pipe,
And sucked at it.

He thought of his victuals,
Of ships, the sea,
Of his home in the West,
And his children three.

And he stared and stared
To where, afar,
The lighthouse gleamed
At the harbour bar;

Till his pipe grew cold,
And down on the board
He laid his head,
And snored, snored, snored.

Very old are the woods;
  And the buds that break
Out of the brier's boughs,
  When March winds wake,
So old with their beauty are –
  Oh, no man knows
Through what wild centuries
  Roves back the rose.

Very old are the brooks;
  And the rills that rise
Where snow sleeps cold beneath
  The azure skies
Sing such a history
  Of come and gone,
Their every drop is as wise
  As Solomon.

Very old are we men;
  Our dreams are tales
Told in dim Eden
  By Eve's nightingales;
We wake and whisper awhile,
  But, the day gone by,
Silence and sleep like fields
  Of amaranth lie.

King Canute
    Sat down by the sea,
Up washed the tide
    And away went he.

Good King Alfred
    Cried, 'My sakes!
Not five winks,
    And look at those cakes!'

Lackland John
    Were a right royal Tartar
Till he made his mark
    Upon *Magna Carta*:

Ink, seal, table,
    On Runnymede green,
Anno Domini
    12 – 15.

The sea washes England,
Where all men speak
A language rich
As ancient Greek.

The wide world over
Man with man
Has talked his own tongue
Since speech began.

Yet still must sorrow
Move the mind,
He understands
But his own kind.

The voices lovely,
Hollow, drear,
Of beast and bird
Beat on his ear:

Eye into eye
Gaze deep he may;
Yet still through Babel
Gropes his way.

As we sailed out of London river,
    Sing a lo lay and a lo lay lone,
I heard a Maid sing – 'Come back, never!'
    And a lo lay lone.

Her hair was yellow as sea-maids' hair is,
    Sing a lo lay and a lo lay lone,
And she'd corn for the chicks that are Mother Carey's;
    And a lo lay lone.

Sam Murphy's grog went cold as water,
    Sing a lo lay and a lo lay lone,
And our hearts to our boots went tumbling after:
    And a lo lay lone.

When we're there and back – by gum, we'll see her,
    Sing a lo lay and a lo lay lone,
Buy cheap she may, but she sells de-ar:
    And a lo lay lone.

'PLEASE TO REMEMBER'

Here am I,
A poor old Guy:
Legs in a bonfire,
Head in the sky;

Shoeless my toes,
Wild stars behind,
Smoke in my nose,
And my eye-peeps blind;

Old hat, old straw –
In this disgrace;
While the wildfire gleams
On a mask for face.

Ay, all I am made of
Only trash is;
And soon – soon,
Will be dust and ashes.

NOW ALL THE ROADS

Now all the roads to London Town
Are windy-white with snow;
There's shouting and cursing,
And snortings to and fro;
But when night hangs her hundred lamps,
And the snickering frost-fires creep,
Then still, O; dale and hill, O;
Snow's fall'n deep.
Then still, O; dale and hill, O;
Snow's fall'n deep.

The carter cracks his leathery whip;
The ostler shouts Gee-whoa;
The farm dog grunts and sniffs and snuffs;
Bleat sheep; and cattle blow;
Soon Moll and Nan in dream are laid,
And snoring Dick's asleep;
Then still, O; dale and hill, O;
Snow's fall'n deep.
Then still, O; dale and hill, O;
Snow's fall'n deep.

Down the Hill of Ludgate,
  Up the Hill of Fleet,
To and fro and East and West
  With people flows the street;
Even the King of England
  On Temple Bar must beat
For leave to ride to Ludgate
  Down the hill of Fleet.

Then as Now; and Now as Then,
Spins on this World of Men.
White – Black – Yellow – Red:
They wake, work, eat, play, go to bed.
Black – Yellow – Red – White:
They talk, laugh, weep, dance, morn to night.
Yellow – Red – White – Black:
Sun shines, moon rides, clouds come back.
Red – White – Black – Yellow:
Count your hardest, who could tell o'
The myriads that have come and gone,
Stayed their stay this earth upon,
And vanished then, their labour done?
Sands of the wilderness, stars in heaven,
Solomon could not sum them even:
Then as Now; Now as Then
Still spins on this World of Men.

8
Winter at the Doors of Spring

Wild are the waves when the wind blows;
But fishes in the deep
Live in a world of waters,
Still as sleep.

Wild are the skies when Winter
Roars at the doors of Spring;
But when his lamentation's lulled
Then sweet birds sing.

The sea laments
The livelong day,
Fringing its waste of sand;
Cries back the wind from the whispering shore –
No words I understand;
Yet echoes in my heart a voice,
As far, as near, as these –
The wind that weeps,
The solemn surge
Of strange and lonely seas.

I supped where bloomed the red red rose,
   And a bird in the tree
Looked on my sweet white bread and whistled
     Tunes to me.

And a wasp prowled in the evening light,
   My honey all about;
And the martin to her sun-baked nest
     Swept in and out.

I sat so still in the garden
   That wasp and leaf and bird
Seemed as I dreamed the only things
     That had ever stirred.

THE FEATHER

A feather, a feather! –
I wonder whether
Of Wren? Or Sparrow?
Or poor Cock Robin,
Shot with an arrow?

A learnèd man
Would tell me whether
This airy scrap
Of down – this feather,
Was of Wren, or Sparrow –
From thorn or willow,
Ivy or gorse,
Or grey leafed sallow –
Or poor Cock Robin's,
Shot with an arrow.

The beak nibs in,
A wind-puff blows,
Off and away
The morsel goes,
Tiny, delicate,
Downy, narrow,
Preened and sleek –
The dainty fellow!

So I can't help asking,
Wren? Or Sparrow?
Or – it would fill
My heart with sorrow –
Poor Cock Robin's,
Slain with an arrow?

JENNY WREN

Of all the birds that rove and sing,
　　Near dwellings made for men,
None is so nimble, feat, and trim
　　　　As Jenny Wren.

With pin-point bill, and a tail a-cock,
　　So wildly shrill she cries,
The echoes on their roof-tree knock
　　　　And fill the skies.

Never was sweeter seraph hid
　　Within so small a house –
A tiny, inch-long, eager, ardent,
　　　　Feathered mouse.

THE SNOWFLAKE

Before I melt,
Come, look at me!
This lovely icy filigree!
Of a great forest
In one night
I make a wilderness
Of white:
By skyey cold
Of crystals made,
All softly, on
Your finger laid,
I pause, that you
My beauty see:
Breathe, and I vanish
Instantly.

ARITHMETIC

There twittering swallows, hawking between the ricks –
The oddest theirs of all arithmetics!

Daring their fears, the cliffs of England won,
Two in late April came . . . Their housework done
They conned this simple problem – (1×1).

And lo! – in the evening sunshine, gilding the ricks –
Four fish-tailed fledgelings, and the answer – six!

THESE SOLEMN HILLS

These solemn hills are silent now that night
Steals softly their green valleys out of sight;
The only sound that through the evening wells
   Is new-born lambkin's bleat;
   And – with soft rounded wings,
   Silvered in day's last light,
      As on they beat –
   The lapwings' slow, sad, anguished
      Pee-oo-eet.

NO BED

No bed! no bed! we shouted,
And wheeled our eyes from home
To where the green and golden woods
    Cried, Come!

Wild sang the evening birds,
The sun-clouds shone in our eyes,
A silver snippet of moon hung low
    In the skies.

We ran, we leapt, we sang,
We yodelled loud and shrill,
Chased Nobody through the valley and
    Up the hill.

We laughed, we quarrelled, we drank
The cool sweet of the dew,
Beading on bud and leaf the dim
    Woods through.

We stayed, we listened, we looked –
Now dark was on the prowl!
Too-whit-a-woo, from its hollow called
    An owl. . . .

O Sleep, at last to slide
Into eyes made drunk with light;
Call in thy footsore boys to harmless
    Night!

A GOLDFINCH

This feather-soft creature
Tail to head,
Is golden yellow,
And black, and red.

A sip of water,
A twig to sing on,
A prong for nest,
The air to wing on,

A mate to love,
Some thistledown seed
Are all his joy, life,
Beauty, need.

No breath of wind,
No gleam of sun –
Still the white snow
Whirls softly down –
Twig and bough
And blade and thorn
All in an icy
Quiet, forlorn.
Whispering, rustling,
Through the air,
On sill and stone,
Roof – everywhere,
It heaps its powdery
Crystal flakes,
Of every tree
A mountain makes;
Till pale and faint
At shut of day,
Stoops from the West
One wintry ray.
And, feathered in fire,
Where ghosts the moon,
A robin shrills
His lonely tune.

Once it made music, tiny, frail, yet sweet –
Bead-note of bird where earth and elfland meet.
Now its thin tinkling stirs no more, since she
Whose toy it was, has gone; and taken the key.

9

Secret Laughter

ECHO
MELMILLO
LONGLEGS
TILLIE
THE RIDE-BY-NIGHTS
NEVER
A WIDOW'S WEEDS
THE STORM
THE BUCKLE
ALL THE WAY
BLUEBELLS
EDEN
THE QUARTETTE

ECHO

'Who called?' I said, and the words
   Through the whispering glades,
Hither, thither, baffled the birds –
   'Who called? Who called?'

The leafy boughs on high
   Hissed in the sun;
The dark air carried my cry
   Faintingly on:

Eyes in the green, in the shade,
    In the motionless brake,
Voices that said what I said,
    For mockery's sake:

'Who cares?' I bawled through my tears;
    The wind fell low:
In the silence, 'Who cares? Who cares?'
    Wailed to and fro.

MELMILLO

Three and thirty birds there stood
In an elder in a wood;
Called Melmillo – flew off three,
Leaving thirty in a tree;
Called Melmillo – nine now gone,
And the boughs held twenty-one;
Called Melmillo – and eighteen
Left but three to nod and preen;
Called Melmillo – three – two – one
Now of birds were feathers none.

Then stole slim Melmillo in
To that wood all dusk and green,
And with lean long palms outspread
Softly a strange dance did tread;
Not a note of music she
Had for echoing company;
All the birds were flown to rest
In the hollow of her breast;
In the wood – thorn, elder, willow –
Danced alone – lone danced Melmillo.

LONGLEGS

Longlegs – he yelled 'Coo-ee!'
  And all across the combe
Shrill and shrill it rang – rang through
  The clear green gloom.

Fairies there were a-spinning,
  And a white tree-maid
Lifted her eyes, and listened
  In her rain-sweet glade.

Bunnie to bunnie stamped; old Wat
  Chin-deep in bracken sate;
A throstle piped, 'I'm by, I'm by!'
  Clear to his timid mate.

And there was Longlegs straddling,
  And hearkening was he,
To distant Echo thrilling back
  A thin 'Coo-ee!'

Old Tillie Turveycombe
Sat to sew,
Just where a patch of fern did grow;
There, as she yawned,
And yawn wide did she,
Floated some seed
Down her gull-e-t;
And look you once,
And look you twice,
Poor old Tillie
Was gone in a trice.
But oh, when the wind
Do a-moaning come,
'Tis poor old Tillie
Sick for home;
And oh, when a voice
In the mist do sigh,
Old Tillie Turveycombe's
Floating by.

THE RIDE-BY-NIGHTS

Up on their brooms the Witches stream,
Crooked and black in the crescent's gleam;
One foot high, and one foot low,
Bearded, cloaked, and cowled, they go.

'Neath Charlie's Wane they twitter and tweet,
And away they swarm 'neath the Dragon's feet,
With a whoop and a flutter they swing and sway,
And surge pell-mell down the Milky Way.

Between the legs of the glittering Chair
They hover and squeak in the empty air.
Then round they swoop past the glimmering Lion
To where Sirius barks behind huge Orion;
Up, then, and over to wheel amain
Under the silver, and home again.

'Take me, or leave me – I'm not thine,'
The fairy mocked on the sands of Lyne –

Frail as Phosphor over the sea –
'Seven long years shalt thou toil for me.'

Full seven I laboured, teen and tine:
But – 'Take me, or leave me, I'm not thine!'

A WIDOW'S WEEDS

A poor Widow in her weeds
Sowed her gardens with wild-flower seeds
Not too shallow, and not too deep;
And down came April – drip – drip – drip.
Up shone May, like gold, and soon
Green as an arbour grew leafy June.

And now all summer she sits and sews
Where willow, herb, confrey, bygloss blows,
Teasel and tansy, meadowsweet,
Campion, toadflax, and rough hawksbit;
Brown bee orchis, and Peals of Bells;
Clover, burnet, and thyme she smells.

Like Oberon's meadows her garden is
Drowsy from dawn to dusk with bees.
Weeps she never, but sometimes sighs,
And peeps at her garden with bright brown eyes;
And all she has is all she needs –
A poor old Widow in her weeds.

THE STORM

First there were two of us, then there were three of us,
Then there was one bird more,
Four of us – wild white sea-birds,
Treading the ocean floor;
And the *wind* rose, and the *sea* rose,
To the angry billows' roar –
With one of us – two of us – three of us – four of us –
Sea-birds on the shore.

Soon there were five of us, soon there were nine of us,
And lo! in a trice sixteen!
And the yeasty surf curdled over the sands,
The gaunt grey rocks between;
And the tempest raved, and the lightning's fire
Struck blue on the spindrift hoar –
And on four of us – ay, and on four times four of us
Sea-birds on the shore.

And our sixteen waxed to thirty-two,
And they to past three score –
A wild, white welter of winnowing wings,
And ever more and more;
And the winds lulled, and the sea went down,
And the sun streamed out on high,
Gilding the pools and the spume and the spars
'Neath the vast blue deeps of the sky;

And the isles and the bright green headlands shone,
As they'd never shone before,
Mountains and valleys of silver cloud,
Wherein to swing, sweep, soar –
A host of screeching, scolding, scrabbling
Sea-birds on the shore –
A snowy, silent, sun-washed drift
Of sea-birds on the shore.

THE BUCKLE

I had a silver buckle,
I sewed it on my shoe,
And 'neath a sprig of mistletoe
I danced the evening through!

I had a bunch of cowslips,
I hid 'em in a grot,
In case the elves should come by night
And me remember not.

I had a yellow riband,
I tied it in my hair,
That, walking in the garden,
The birds might see it there.

I had a secret laughter,
I laughed it near the wall:
Only the ivy and the wind
May tell of it at all.

ALL THE WAY

All the way from Adam
You came, my dear, to me;
The wind upon your cheek
Wafted Noah on the sea,
The daisy in your hand –
Silver petals, stud of gold –
Just such another starred the grass,
   In Eden, of old.

It's a long, long way to Abel,
And a path of thorns to Cain,
And men less wise than Solomon
Must tread them both again;
But those fountains still are spouting,
And the Serpent twines the bough,
And lovely Eve is sleeping
   In our orchard, *now*.

BLUEBELLS

Where the bluebells and the wind are,
　　Fairies in a ring I spied,
And I heard a little linnet
　　Singing near beside.

Where the primrose and the dew are,
　　Soon were sped the fairies all:
Only now the green turf freshens,
　　And the linnets call.

EDEN

I wonder if from Noah's Ark
Ever was heard the bobtail's bark.
If ever o'er the empty Flood
Our English ash-boughs stood in bud.
'Tis sure when Eve and Adam sate
Smiling within green Eden's gate
And gave its birds, beasts, fishes, names
Somewhere flowed clear our English Thames.

And when they both in woe were driven
Beyond the shining bounds of heaven,
Simply for grief that outcast morn
Broke into bloom our English thorn.
And – far from Eden – our nightingale
Did their sad banishment bewail;
While we, asleep within her dust,
Hearkened – as all poor humans must.

Tom sang for joy, and Ned sang for joy and old Sam sang
for joy;
All we four boys piped up loud, just like one boy;
And the ladies that sate with the Squire – their cheeks were
all wet,
For the noise of the voice of us boys, when we sang our
Quartette.

Tom he piped low, and Ned he piped low, and old Sam
he piped low;
Into a sorrowful fall did our music flow;
And the ladies that sate with the Squire vowed they'd never
forget
How the eyes of them cried for delight, when we sang our
Quartette.

Index of First Lines